Naples

FLORIDA

a photographic portrait

Other titles by PilotPress Publishers, Inc., and Twin Lights Publishers

Cape Ann: A Photographic Portrait
Greater Newburyport: A Photographic Portrait
Kittery to the Kennebunks: A Photographic Portrait
The White Mountains: A Photographic Portrait
Portsmouth and Coastal New Hampshire: A Photographic Portrait
The Mystic Coast, Stonington to New London: A Photographic Portrait
The Rhode Island Coast: A Photographic Portrait
Upper Cape Cod: A Photographic Portrait
Boston's South Shore: A Photographic Portrait

First published in the United States of America by
PilotPress Publishers, Inc.
110 Weschester Road
Newton, Massachusetts 02458
Telephone: (617) 332-0703
http://www.PilotPress.com

and

Twin Lights Publishers, Inc.
10 Hale Street
Rockport, Massachusetts 01966
Telephone: (978) 546-7398
http://www.twinlightspub.com

ISBN 1-885435-15-0

10 9 8 7 6 5 4 3 2

Book design by
SYP Design & Production
http://www.sypdesign.com

Front Cover Photo by: August Uttich

Printed in China

Contents

Acknowledgments

PilotPress Publishers and Twin Lights Publishers wish to thank all of the photographers who submitted their work for our consideration. Because of space limitations, we were unable to include many excellent photographs in *Naples, Florida: A Photographic Portrait*. The Naples area is a fertile area for many talented resident professional and amateur photographers. The natural beauty attracts visitors to record its special qualities at all times of the year.

Special thanks go to Abbi Goodman and Peter McGee who organized and supervised the photography contest. Their efficiency and thoroughness made the judging of over 600 entries a less difficult task.

Thanks go to the judges of the Naples Regional Photograph Contest, Parker Hathcock, Tim Stamm, and Peter Thomas. We are pleased with their selections and are indebted to them.

Parker Hathcock was recently editor of the local Naples area's "n" Magazine. Tim Stamm is a professional portrait and general photographer working in the Naples region. Peter Thomas is an internationally known narrator who worked for CBS for many years.

We extend our appreciation to Carl Thome for the use of his aerial photographs, the Keewaydin Island Limited Partners for their photographs, and to Nancy Hannigan creator of the map used to describe the area. Our thanks go also to Jackie Frank of the Collier County Historical Society for the use of the old Naples photographs, and to Wynn's Market for their help in hosting the Naples Regional Photographic Contest.

We are grateful to Laura Leydon, a journalist with the Naples Daily News and writer of the captions for the photographs. In writing the captions, she has found evocative titles and added facts to bring out the history and local color for each photograph. We think she has given an added dimension to the book.

Finally, our thanks go to designer Sara Day who has created a beautiful book.

Introduction

A day doesn't pass when Ann Skoluda Hoagland isn't thankful for living in Naples. In addition to sharing her favorite photo for this book she offered the touching words seen below to describe the "magical" place she calls home.

Naples is home to year-rounders and winter residents, many of whom have chosen to buy homes here so they can spend months at a time taking in the area's beauty. Tourists flock to the area all year, though most visitors come during the winter months to escape the icy temperatures up north.

Spectacular sunsets, ocean vistas, sandy beaches, palm-fringed streets, glorious flowers, wildlife, mangroves, wetland preserves. These are just some of Naples' attributes that have inspired this book. We have found Naples to be a beautiful place to live, work and play.

The coastal area has a special appeal to birdwatchers, boaters and fisherman. And of course to golfers. Naples ranks second in the nation based on the number of golf holes per resident, according to the National Golf Foundation in Jupiter, Florida.

Naples: A Photographic Portrait is an attempt to capture for posterity's sake this special place, as seen through the eyes of residents and visitors, who shared their photos.

If you enjoy this photographic portrait and haven't visited the area, we hope you will have a chance to take in Naples' beauty with your own eyes and maybe discover some treasures of your own.

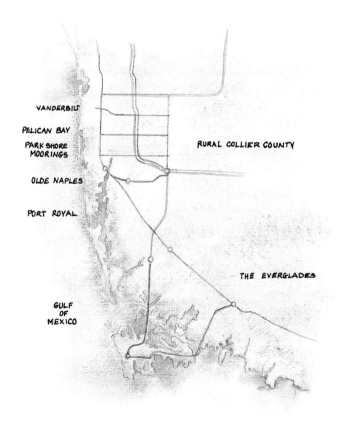

VANDERBILT
PELICAN BAY
PARK SHORE
MOORINGS
OLDE NAPLES
PORT ROYAL
GULF OF MEXICO
RURAL COLLIER COUNTY
THE EVERGLADES

Naples, Florida
Where discoveries abound,
Small treasures and large.
From seashells...
To our inner selves.

© 2000 Ann Skoluda Hoagland

FIRST PRIZE

Sunset at the Naples Pier

AUGUST UTTICH

For August photography has been a longtime hobby. Though he's taken hundreds of photos, the retiree entered just one in the contest, a shot of a spectacular sunset. It was taken at the city's most famous landmark, the Naples Pier. "This is the only one I thought would have the possibility of winning a prize," he told a local reporter at the *Naples Daily News* after learning his photo had taken the top honor. August, a Naples resident, took the picture a few years ago.

SECOND PRIZE

Naples Philharmonic at Night

EUGENE GIBBONS

When Eugene's wife Marilyn learned that his photo won second place in the photo contest, she got so emotional tears welled up in her eyes. Eugene passed away in 1994. Marilyn, a local resident, submitted the photo in his honor. "This means so much that this is going to be in a book," she said, adding that she planned to buy copies of the picture book for her children and grandchildren. Today, Marilyn says, it wouldn't be possible to get this shot because another building blocks the view captured by her husband.

THIRD PRIZE (opposite)

The Great Egret

MARYLE BARBÉ

Maryle, a Bonita Springs resident, loves birds and has been an avid bird-watcher for years. She visits Corkscrew Swamp Sanctuary, where this photo was taken, as often as she can. Maryle considers herself lucky to have found this egret when she did, the magnificent plumage on his back is only there during the breeding season. Like the other winners, Maryle is an amateur photographer. Indeed, she says, she's not taken one class in photography.

1

1 - HONORABLE MENTION

Mellow Yellow

PEGGY PARADISE
NIKON F2
KODAK E100SW
F-4

A summer storm creates a magical glow in the sky. This shot was captured at the Naples Pier, considered the most perfect spot for sunset-gazers.

2 - HONORABLE MENTION (*opposite*)

Seminole Son

JUDY CASELEY

Dressed up in tribal garb, a young boy shares his culture with onlookers on Seminole Indian Day, held every year at Smallwood's Store and Museum on Chokoloskee. In past years, activities have included a mullet toss and a best-dressed contest.

2

Shop 'Til You Drop

ROGER DEVORE
FUJI G617 PANORAMIC
FUJI PROVIA TRANSPARENCY FILM
F–22, 2 MINUTES

The beach isn't the only attraction for visitors. In 1999, Naples was voted second only to Myrtle Beach, South Carolina in the amount of retail space it has per resident. In some years, it has taken the top spot thanks to centers like The Village on Venetian Bay pictured above. At night, the center creates a rainbow of lights on the bay.

PORT ROYAL
OLD NAPLES

1

2
3

1

Fishing Club

COURTESY OF KEEWAYDIN ISLAND
LIMITED PARTNERS

A classic yacht brings visitors to
the historic Keeywadin Club on
Keeywadin Island. The only way
to get to the island is by boat.

2

Island Adventure

COURTESY OF KEEWAYDIN ISLAND
LIMITED PARTNERS

An aerial shows the stark contrast
between Port Royal and Keeywadin
Island, which are linked by Gordon
Pass. The island, stretching seven
miles in length, has seen record
breaking sales in recent years.

3

Pelican Pile-Up

ARLENE TALIADOROS

Pelicans line up on pilings, after
a day of fishing.

1

1

Ready for a Spin

JOHN CICILLINE
LEICA M5
FUJI

This classic car stirs up memories of bygone days. Every year, an antique car show is held in Old Naples, giving owners a chance to show off vintage cars like this old Mercedes Benz.

2

Charming Church

ANGELA ANTILIA
KALIMAR KX 5000 SLR
FUJI SLIDE FILM

Here's the window. Here's the fence. Look inside, and you'll see the charm that brings parishioners back to the Port Royal Episcopal Church every Sunday.

2

1

The White House

FRED WICKE
NIKON N 70
SEATTLECHROME 100

Though the president of the United States does not live in Port Royal, the area has attracted retired presidents and chief executive officers of several Fortune 500 companies. This home reflects off bright blue waters, creating a postcard image.

2

Millionaires and Mansions

JERRY SHELTON
MINOLTA MAXXUM 7000
KODAK 150 100 AUTO

A drive around Port Royal is always dazzling. Home after home has been torn down, making way for some of Naples' most graceful residences.

3

Mirror Image

WANDA SOLON
KODAK 35 MM 200 SPEED

Boats reflect in a canal off Third Street South, where some of Naples' finest restaurants and shops are located.

2

3

1

Painting the Town Red

SAMUEL HUNKIN II
OLYMPUS STYLUS SINGLE LENS REFLEX
WALGREEN'S 400 SPEED

With clouds painted across the sky, Mother Nature puts on another spectacular sunset at the Naples Pier.

2

Catching a Wave

PAUL STEVENS
NIKON F3AF
DISPOSABLE
NIKON - FUJI

Peter Stevens shows off for his dad at a Naples Beach. There were some "killer" waves that day, at least by Naples' standards.

3

Setting Sun

LEE WARNER
CANON AE – 1
KODAK 400 AUTOMATIC

Yet another beautiful sunset in Naples. The photo was shot at Naples Beach at the end of Fifth Avenue South, one of Naples' oldest streets.

1

2

3

1

Private Party

WANDA SOLON
MINOLTA KODAK 35 MM 200 SPEED

Add wine and cheese and a blanket and this is the perfect spot for an afternoon picnic. The rocks overlook Gordon Pass, a boating haven.

2

Pelicans in a Row

GINNY FOLK
CANON FTB FULLY MANUAL
KODAK GOLD 200 SPEED, COLOR
F–5.6, SHUTTER 60

Drifting with the tide, pelicans glide through the gulf. It's as if they were playing follow the leader.

3

City Dock

CAROLINE BROWN
135 MM

Keeping a watchful eye on his surroundings, a pelican glides effortlessly through the water at the Naples City Dock.

(following page)

A Boy and His Truck

CAROLINE BROWN
NIKON N 90 80 – 210
POLARIZER FILTER

As the sun sets at a public beach in Naples, a boy's imagination runs wild. The beach becomes an interstate highway to transport his truck to the next town.

1

Tin City

GARY SHULTZ

The nautical nature of Tin City makes it one of Naples' most popular attractions. Spanning more than 23,000 square feet, it was Naples' first waterfront shopping center. There are more than 40 boutiques and restaurants, including the Riverwalk Fish & Ale House and Merriman's Wharf.

2

Red Sky at Night

ROBERT BRADFORD

As the sun sets across the mainsail of a yacht, the crew looks on with admiration. This photo was snapped at 10th Avenue South, a few blocks from the Naples Pier.

3

Gone Fishin'

ARLENE TALIADOROS

In Naples, it's no secret fishing is a favorite pastime. Even Hollywood recognizes that fact. In 1995, 'Gone Fishin', starring Danny Glover, Joe Pesci and Roseanna Arquette, was shot in and around Naples.

1

2

3

1

"Satchmo"

FRED WICKE
NIKON N 70
SEATTLECHROME 100
3.8 – 11, WITH BRACKETING

Louis Armstrong was found playing his trumpet on Third Street South, known as gallery row. His statue was visiting the street, which is lined with art galleries, shops, and resturants.

2

Fish or Famine

FRED WICKE
NIKON N 70
SEATTLECHROME 100

Fishing poles in bright hues eagerly await the start of the Kid's Fishing Clinic, an annual event at the Naples Pier. In Naples, fishing is fun at any age.

3

White or Wheat?

MARIAN HAMMOND
MINOLTA X370, 100 ASA 50 M, F8-125

Located in one of the more historic buildings in Naples, Fantozzi's Café boasts the best deli sandwich in Naples. The Olde Naples Building, which dates back to the 1920s, was Naple's first office building

1

2

1

Coming in for a Landing

CAROLINE BROWN
OLYMPUS OM 1, 50 MM

A pelican appears ready for a safe
landing at the Naples Pier. Developers
have fought over the rights to use the
bird's name in Southwest Florida. Pelican Landing, Pelican Bay and Pelican
Marsh are just a few of the communi-
ties in the region that bear the name.

2

Yakety Yak

JERRY SHELTON
MINOLTA MAXXUM 7000
KODAK 150 100 AUTO

Feathered friends catch up on old
times, as they meet at the Naples
Pier. Soon, they'll move on, with hope
that they'll see each other again.

3

Fit for a Queen

DEBORAH BOROWSKI
CANON REBEL, G905
KODAK MAX 800

It seems a moat is all that's needed
to make this castle good enough
for royalty. Sculptures like these
can be found nearly every day at
the beach.

3

1

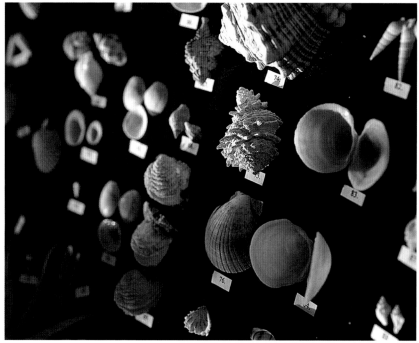

2
3

1 & 2

Treasure Hunt

COURTESY OF KEEWAYDIN ISLAND
LIMITED PARTNERS

Visitors come from near and far to
search for treasure along the shores
of Keeywadin Island. A guided tour
of the quaint island includes a
shelling bag. Conchs, tulips and
sand dollars are just a few of the
shells found on the island.

3

Who Goes There?

CAROLINE BROWN
OLYMPUS OM 1
135 MM LENS

Traces of life are left in the sand.
But whom these footprints belong
to remains a mystery.

Life's a Beach

RYVANNE SUSSER
KODAK ADVANTIX 4100 IX ZOOM
KODAK ADVANTIX – 200 AUTO

Some beachgoers take a dip in
calm waters along the Old Naples
shoreline, while others catch up on
much needed rest.

1

2

3

1

At Ease

RYVANNE SUSSER
KODAK ADVANTIX 4100 IX ZOOM
KODAK ADVANTIX 200 AUTO

With clouds looming overhead, boaters call it an early day.

2

Nap Time

MARIAN HAMMOND
MINOLTA X 370
100 ASA
50 M F-8 – 250

Boats take a rest on a chilly day in January at the City Dock, home to Naples' largest charter fishing fleet. As soon as it's warm again, the municipal dock will be hopping.

3

Against the Wind

WILLIAM WARD MOSELEY
NIKON 8008
KODAK GOLD 200/ 60 MM
F-22

A burgee blows gently in the wind, while sails take a much-needed rest.

1

2

Water Logged

NANCY THURSTON
CANON AE – 1 PROGRAM
KODAK GOLD 200 F-16

After a long journey, driftwood dries itself out at the Naples Beach.

Cast a Net

CATHERINE CHRISTIAN
KODAK DISPOSABLE
35 MM

A tourist gets a lesson on how to use a cast net to collect bait in waters off Keeywaydin Island. The instructor reiterates, "practice makes perfect."

1

1	2	3	4
### Home Made	### Ready to Hunt	### Roaring '20s	### Naples Undiscovered
COURTESY OF THE COLLIER COUNTY HISTORICAL SOCIETY	COURTESY OF COLLIER COUNTY HISTORICAL SOCIETY	COURTESY OF COLLIER COUNTY HISTORICAL SOCIETY	COURTESY OF COLLIER COUNTY HISTORICAL SOCIETY
Palm Cottage, Naples' second oldest existing home, was built with home made concrete known as Tabbie Mortar for Henry Watterson, famed editor of the Louisville Courier-Journal. Pictured here are Mr. and Mrs. Walter O. Parmer, who owned the house from 1916 to 1938.	In this 1947 photo, "Ed" Frank, inventor of the Swamp Buggy, is about to head out for a weeklong hunting trip with his buddies in the Everglades. Paul Frank and Henry Espenlaub stand on his left, Naples Mayor Roy Smith is on the right.	Reproduced from a postcard, this panoramic photo shows the Old Naples Hotel at its prime in the 1920s. It is the only full view of the hotel known to exist.	As this aerial shows, Old Naples' beauty was still a well-kept secret in 1958. In those days, getting around town was a breeze and there was plenty of land to build on. A building boom has changed that.

2

3

4

1
2

1

Bird Bath

CAROLINE BROWN
NIKON N90, 80-210 LENS

A royal tern grooms himself in the sun's glow at the Naples Beach.

2

Picture Perfect

TIM ZELLO
NIKON
100 SPEED FILM, F-4

Framed by palm trees, the shoreline hosts an exquisite sunset, near Third Street South in Naples.

Birds in Flight

EDIE PENNOYER VASSAMILLET
OLYMPUS ZOOM
KODAK 200
MULTI AF

Birds dance across the sky, as a lazy
day at the beach comes to an end.

Faded Glory

KAY PATTON
CANON EOS
FUJI COLOR SUPERIA 200 SPEED
125 AT F-5.6

The sun fades away, ushering in
another night in paradise.

Setting Sail

LAWRENCE TOMSIC
OLYMPUS INFINITY SUPER ZOOM 300
KODAK 100
F-11 AT 1/125 SEC.

Undeterred by clouds, a crew sails across the Gulf of Mexico, near the Naples Pier. In the background is the Wilkinson House, one of Naples' oldest residences. Located on 9th Street South, the home is owned by the Collier County Historical Society and was home to Naples' first elected mayor, Edwards Wilkinson.

Street Art

JOHN CICILLINE
LEICA M5
FUJI

A Mainstreet Art program has put an array of statues on sidewalks along Naples' Main Street. It's another step in the renewal of Fifth Avenue South, one of Naples' oldest streets.

Here I Come

ANDY SPOONER
OLYMPUS D 400 ZOOM
DIGITAL AUTO

Gulls are startled into flight, as
two-year-old Erin Spooner races
to greet them, running toward the
Naples Pier.

Sunblock

CAROLINE BROWN
NIKON N 90
KODAK ROYAL GOLD AND FUJI VELVIA

Who needs greasy sunscreen, when you've got an umbrella like this? It's big enough for the whole family. Without it, chances are you'll burn, especially on a summer day.

1

Church by the Sea

WANDA SOLON
KODAK 35 MM 200 SPEED

The Trinity-By-The-Cove, an episcopal church built in 1958, is within a few miles of the Gulf of Mexico. On one Sunday a year, parishioners can look out the window during service and see runners competing in the Naples Daily News Half Marathon. The marathon winds through Old Naples, finishing at Cambier Park.

2

Quaint Cottage

WANDA SOLON
MINOLTA
KODAK 35 MM, 200 SPEED

Palm Cottage, located on 12th Avenue South, was the first house to be acquired by the Collier County Historical Society, but not the last. The society also owns the Wilkinson House, an old plantation-style house on 9th Street South that historians believe was built in 1914.

3

Anyone Home?

WANDA SOLON
MINOLTA
KODAK, 35 MM, 200 SPEED

Warm and cozy. That's what makes some of Naples' older homes so inviting. The gate is open, as if to say, "C'mon in."

2

3

1

2

1

All Aboard

WANDA SOLON
MINOLTA
KODAK 35 MM 200 SPEED

A train whistle still blows at the Naples Depot. It's heard every day at noon. The depot, now used for meetings and other local events, is listed on the National Register of Historical Places.

2

At the Center of Art

WANDA SOLON
MINOLTA
KODAK 35 MM 200 SPEED

The Von Liebig Art Center, home to the Naples Art Association, has been called a "real jewel" in Collier County. In the center's first eight months, it saw more than 30,000 people come through its doors. The center has the largest collection of art books in the county.

3

Pride and Joy

CAROLYNE JOHNSTONE
OLYMPUS OM – 10
KODAK
F-16

Emily Donnery gives her grandmother a grin, while sitting on pilings at 32nd Avenue. The duo shared more than just a hat. They spent a day at the beach, searching for shells and wading in warm gulf waters.

3

1

2
3

Sounds of Music

WANDA SOLON
MINOLTA
KODAK 35 MM 200 SPEED

Ears are filled with delightful music at Cambier Park in Old Naples. On stage is the Naples Concert Band, which has performed for more than a quarter of a century.

Chalk Art

WANDA SOLON

Kodak 35 mm 200 Speed

An aspiring artist shows off her talents at a Chalk Art Festival. The event is held every year along Fifth Avenue South, Naples' main street.

Summer Solace

WANDA SOLON
KODAK 35 MM 200 SPEED

Add a cold glass of lemonade and the company of a good friend, and you've got the perfect summertime hangout. The gazebo, on 13th Avenue South, is a stone's throw from the beach.

1

2

1

Alone At Last

NANCY HANNIGAN
OLYMPUS ED 35 – 180
KODAK 200 ASA AUTO

Boats appear to have the beach to themselves in this photo of an artist's rendering. No telling when their captains will return.

2

Swan Court

NANCY HANNIGAN
OLYMPUS ED 35 – 180
KODAK 200 ASA AUTO

On a cool day, this courtyard at the Mercantile building in Old Naples is a favorite eating spot. The courtyard's beauty, no doubt, inspires its name. And it's what inspired this painting by Nancy Hannigan.

Scratch 'N Sniff

NANCY HANNIGAN
OLYMPUS ED 35 – 180
KODAK 200 ASA AUTO

In Naples, flowers bloom all
year-round, giving this artist plenty
to work with from January to
December. These plumerias are so
lifelike, you can almost smell their
sweet aroma.

1

1

Old Marine Market Place

CARL THOME

These buildings date back to the 1920s, and once housed a clam shelling and processing plant. Today, the waterfront center, more popularly known as Tin City, is home to many sightseeing boats and fishing vessels.

2

Cottage Art

NANCY HANNIGAN
OLYMPUS ED 35 – 180
KODAK 200 ASA AUTO

Nancy Hannigan uses watercolors to bring the Palm Cottage to life. The cottage, built in 1895, is now the headquarters of the Collier County Historical Society.

3

Cracker House

NANCY HANNIGAN
OLYMPUS ED 35 – 180
KODAK 200 ASA AUTO

This Old Naples house is quaint, yet charming. This is one of Hannigan's favorite paintings. The artist owns a studio in Old Naples, and paints ceramic tile on location. "I've been painting all my life," she says.

2

3

1

2

1	2	3

Soaring

SUZY MAYNARD
CANON EOS REBEL
KODAK
F-6-8

A seagull followed this photographer, a winter resident, for three or four minutes, hovering just six feet above her head. "It had never happened to me before," Suzy recalls. "I fumbled through my camera bag to get a shot."

Treasure Trove

CYNTHIA CRONIG
MINOLTA 400 SI
KODAK GOLD 100 ISO F–11

The sea beckons young and old to enjoy its treasures. Here, yet another sunset is celebrated at the Naples Pier, Naples' most famous landmark. It's not unusual to hear applause by spectators when the sun disappears in the horizon.

Early Retirement

JODI LYNN LESKO

Who says you have to be retired to enjoy the beach? Not this youngster, who took an afternoon nap at the beach.

3

THE MOORINGS
PARK SHORE

1

1

Backyard Beauty

HELEN STALLARD
VIVITAR SERIES 1
KODAK 400

While the Naples Pier is known as "the place" to watch a sunset in Naples, residents lucky enough to live on Gulf Shore Boulevard, can witness spectacular sunsets from their own backyards.

2

Fore!

LYNNE REDMOND
OLYMPUS
KODAK FILM
AUTO FOCUS

An egret evaluates golfers as they tee-off at a local golf course. Golf courses in Naples have hosted many tournaments including Naples' Seniors PGA.

3

Lone Ranger

LYNN ROYAL
OLYMPUS INFINITY TWIN
KODAK 200 35 MM

A pelican takes in a spectacular sunset along the beach. It appears the bird has the beach to himself for a change.

2

3

1

2

3

1

On the Rocks

CHRISTA JAEGERS
MINOLTA – VEC TIS 20
KODAK GOLD 200 FILM

Waves crash onto magnificent rock formations, while a feathered friend keeps a watchful eye on the shoreline. The water is a little chilly for fishing on this winter day.

2

Seagate Beach

DIANA NELL

On a windy day, a sailboat cuts across choppy waters at Seagate Beach.

3

Heavenly Sun

BARBARA WENDERSKI

A glorious sun peaks through the clouds, creating a reflection in the gulf. In front, waves crash ashore.

1

1

Bridge with a View

DIANA NELL

Calm waters greet boaters on a magnificently clear day. A local resident captured this photo while standing on the Moorings Line Drive bridge.

2

Tree Tops

RYVANNE SUSSER
KODAK ADVANTIX 4100 IX ZOOM
KODAK ADVANTIX 200

Beautiful tree-lined streets capture the attention of tourists. A California resident visiting the area shot this photo on a cool afternoon in November.

3

Pot of Gold

CHRISTA JAEGERS
MINOLTA – VEC TIS 20
KODAK GOLD 200 FILM

An afternoon rainstorm brings with it a magnificent rainbow at Emerald Lakes. The colors are reflected off a lake in the development.

2

3

1

2
3

1

Rain or Shine

DEHLIA HURST
NIKON N 70
FUJI 200, F-16

Shops and restaurants reflect off the water in the Venetian Bay, as the noon hour approaches. Even on a sunny day like this shoppers come to The Village on Venetian Bay to check out what's new and different.

2

A Shopping Village

CHRISTA JAEGERS
MINOLTA – VEC TIS 20
KODAK GOLD 200 FILM

Palm trees line the entrance to The Village on Venetian Bay. The center is reminiscent of a European village.

3

Table for Two

WANDA SOLON
KODAK 35 MM 200 SPEED

Charming tables invite visitors to dine outdoors at The Village on Venetian Bay. Wrought iron tables and park benches are perfect spots to enjoy a cappuccino or gourmet ice cream.

1

2

3

1

Shadow Dancing

CARL STOYE

The sun casts shadows on a brick walkway that greets visitors at The Village on Venetian Bay. Palm trees and other lush trees surround the village, a favorite shopping spot for visitors and residents.

2

Misty Morning

MARILYN HARRIS
OLYMPUS 35 MM
KODAK 400 SPEED AUTOMATIC

Fog isn't enough to chase these fishermen away. Lines are cast in Moorings Bay, with hopes of catching mullet. Some locals consider these fish "good eating," while others use them only for bait.

3

Jungle Larry's

WANDA SOLON
KODAK 35 MM 200 SPEED

A wooden bridge takes visitors across a pond filled with tropical fish and plants to the entrance of Naples' only zoo. The attraction's formal name is Caribbean Gardens, but locals know it as Jungle Larry's. At the 52-acre park, you'll find everything from alligators to zebras.

1

2

1

Who's the Fairest of Them All?

GINNY FOLK
CANON FTB, FULLY MANUAL
KODAK GOLD, 200 SPEED
F–22, SHUTTER 500

Palms admire themselves in tinted glass at the Northern Trust Bank in North Naples. Naples is home to dozens of banking institutions, all here to compete for their share of the wealth in Naples.

2

Round He Goes

BABS ARMOUR

An egret circles a pond in hopes of finding something to munch on. The red and pink flowers in the foreground are a stark contrast to the snowy-white bird, which is found lurking near water in Naples.

3

A Sign of Spring

LAWRENCE W. TOMSIC
OLYMPUS SUPER ZOOM 300
KODAK 100 , F-11, 1/125 SEC

When the yellow Tabebuia Caraiba, or Golden Trumpet tree, blooms it's a sure sign that spring has arrived. While the flowers are magnificent to look at, they fall on otherwise well manicured lawns, causing their owners headaches.

3

1

2

Sunset Duet

GENE CLAYTON
OLYMPUS OM 2N
KODAK ROYAL GOLD 200
F–22 AT 1/125

Even as the sun sets across the gulf, this couple seems determined not to go home empty handed. The duo was fishing at Lowdermilk Park. If you turn the picture on its side, you'll discover a map of Florida, framed by ominous clouds. The photo won an Editors Choice Award, given out by the International Library of Photography.

1

Ripple Effect

GERRY SUGARMAN

On a warm Christmas morning, a local resident got a present he didn't expect, a perfect setting for a perfect photo of this sand-rippled beach.

2

Something's Fishy

LYNNE REDMOND
OLYMPUS
KODAK
AUTO FOCUS

A blue heron stands proud, as waves crash nearby. Herons are birds of prey, feeding primarily on fish.

1

Sun's Rays and Clouds

ANN SKOLUDA HOAGLAND

Beach grass, sand, sea, clouds, and the sun's rays combine to create a magical moment at Park Shore Beach.

2

Cruising by Land and Sea

JERRY SHELTON
MINOLTA MAXXUM 7000
KODAK 150 100 AUTO

While Doctor Pass is a popular cruising spot for boaters, nearby you'll often see runners speeding down Gulf Shore Boulevard, probably in training for their next marathon.

PELICAN BAY
NORTH NAPLES

1

2

3

1

Safe at Home

SAMUEL HUNKIN II
OLYMPUS STYLUS SINGLE LENS REFLEX
WALGREEN'S 400 SPEED

A summer storm keeps Pelican Bay residents from venturing to the beach. Unlike humans, the beach chairs have no choice but to weather the storm. When the county approved the Pelican Bay development in 1977 it was the largest development in Naples and it was expected to have a larger population than the city.

2

Is That Me?

CAROLINE BROWN
NIKON N-90
80-210 2X CONVERTER

An Ibis takes a nosedive in search of dinner, creating a mirror image in the water. The bird was fishing in Pelican Bay.

3

Taking a Load Off

ARLENE TALIADOROS
NIKON N-90
FUJI 100

Pelicans rest on old pilings at a Naples Beach. Locals can't seem to get enough of this fabulous bird. They are an inspiration to artists and photographers alike.

(following page)

Brave Souls

SAMUEL HUNKIN II
OLYMPUS STYLUS SINGLE LENS REFLEX
WALGREEN'S 400 SPEED

Storm clouds chase some beach-goers away, while others are determined to stay.

1	2	3

In Hiding

ED DONALDSON
MINOLTA VELTIS 30
KODAK ADVANTIX AUTO PANORAMIC

A wall of clouds shields the sun as its sets on Pelican Bay. Clouds like this often fill the sky during the summer months. While rain is not welcomed by tourists, locals thirst for it and need it to restore their fresh water supply. In Naples, a drought can last for months at a time.

Flash Photography

SAMUEL HUNKIN II
OLYMPUS STYLUS SINGLE LENS REFLEX
WALGREEN'S 400 SPEED

Hundreds of photographers have tried to capture this green flash on film. But few have done it. This photographer had his equipment ready. He snapped the photo just as the sun appeared to touch the ocean.

Waterside Shops

GARY SHULTZ

Cascading waterfalls calm shoppers at the Waterside Shops. The enchanting center features well-known fashion stores and specialty shops, such as Williams-Sonoma and Crabtree & Evelyn. Waterside also has five restaurants, including Silver Spoon Café and California Pizza Kitchen.

1

1

Double Vision

LENORA RICKNER

Lenora Rickner admires her grandchildren as she sits near the shoreline at Vanderbilt Beach. Dressed in
their Sunday's best, the girls frol-
icked in unusually warm waters on
a February afternoon.

2

Something to Remember

CAROLINE BROWN
NIKON – 90 80-22 LENS

Tourists enjoy a sunset along the
beach in North Naples. It seems the
sunset is never the same. For that
reason, year-round residents can
always be caught gazing sunsets in
awe along the Naples shoreline.

2

1

1

Taking a Moment

SAMUEL HUNKIN II
OLYMPUS STYLUS SINGLE LENS REFLEX
WALGREEN'S 400 SPEED

The sun reflects on the water, as a couple thinks back on their day. The two were going for a stroll on the beach, a favorite after dinner activity in Naples.

2

The Phil

CARL STOYE

Voted the "best place to be seen, by "n Magazine," a local publication, the Philharmonic Center for the Arts is a magnet for the who's who of Naples. The center hosts more than 400 events a year, including theater productions such as *Cats* and *The King and I*. It's home to the Naples Philharmonic Orchestra.

3

Lean on Me

SAMUEL HUNKIN II
OLYMPUS STYLUS SINGLE LENS REFLEX
WALGREEN'S 400 SPEED

A palm tree looks for a little support from a stronger neighbor. Its neighbor is happy to oblige.

2

3

RURAL
NAPLES

River of Grass

WANDA SOLON
KODAK 35 MM 200 SPEED

Eco-tours offer airboat rides through the Everglades, a natural river of grass that is being restored with the help of state and federal dollars. Its beauty has not gone unnoticed by Hollywood heavyweights. In 1994, scenes for "Just Cause," starring Sean Connery, were shot in Copeland, a tiny town nestled in the Everglades.

Take Cover

WANDA SOLON
KODAK 35 MM 200 SPEED

Clouds appear to float in the canal, as a storm moves toward Everglades City. The photo was taken from a bridge on Stewart Boulevard off of Everglades Boulevard.

Ten-hut!

JUDY CASELEY

A small army of white pelicans stands at attention, hoping to be fed by a human hand. The pelicans migrate to Southwest Florida in the winter, coming from Canada in search of warmer weather. In Naples, temperatures rarely drop below the 70s.

Trading Places

JUDY CASELEY

Today if you want to make a purchase at Smallwood's Store in Everglades City, you'd better bring cash. But cash wasn't always a requirement for getting merchandise. Established as a trading post in 1906, Smallwood's once bartered hides and farm produce for hard-to-come by items. The store, on the National Register of Historic Places, is now a museum.

1

2 ▸

1

Island Beauty

JOHN CICILLINE
LEICA M5
FUJI

The sun peaks out from a delicate ecosystem in the Everglades, creating a remarkable reflection.

2

On the Boardwalk

CAROLYN HAWKINS
MINOLTA 9X1 50 MM LENS
KODAK 200

A 2-1/4-mile boardwalk winds through several habitats at the National Audubon Society's Corkscrew Swamp Sanctuary. Along the way, you'll see 500-year old cypress trees, ferns, air plants and wildflowers.

1

Florida Gator

DOROTHY SKOLUDA

A baby alligator camouflages himself with lettuce leaves at the Corkscrew Swamp Sanctuary. When there hasn't been much rain, gators move into patches of swampland near the boardwalk, giving visitors a greater chance of seeing them up close.

2

Stumped

WANDA SOLON
KODAK 35 MM 200 SPEED

The mysterious Everglades attracts hundreds of thousands of visitors a year. It supports a diversity of trees, plants and animals, including manatees and eagles. Some lucky visitors have even seen the elusive Florida Panther, a dying breed.

3

Can You, Canoe?

JUDY CASELEY

Seminole Indians go for a spin in a canoe offshore in Everglades City. It is part of the Seminole Day activities on Chokoloskee in the Ten Thousand Islands.

2

1

3

1

2

3

1

The Last of the Canoe Men

JUDY CASELEY

Henry John shows off his master-piece during Seminole Indian Day at Smallwood's Store and Museum on Chokoloskee Island. John, 74, made the traditional Seminole canoe from the core of a hollowed out Cypress log. He claims to be the last in the tribe to know the trade.

2

Soft Reflections

PAUL REINHARDT
APEX APS, 200 SPEED
F – 6.6 AT 1/100 SECONDS

Palm trees reflect in a pond off Riviera Boulevard in East Naples. It was an unusually foggy day. "I thought this was going to make a neat photo," says Reinhardt, an amateur photographer. "So, I drove out to the pond and took it."

3

Last Stand

PETER WAGNER
CANON 285
200

This fruit stand is one of the last of its kind in rural Naples. Citrus, however, remains a vital industry in Southwest Florida. Stoney's, based in Naples, has had groves in the area for decades.

PLANTS AND ANIMALS

1

2

3

(previous pages)

Profusion of Orchids

PAUL STEVENS
NIKON F3AF,
DISPOSABLE, NIKON FUJI

Four different varieties of tropical orchids create a brilliant tapestry of color.

1

Ugly Ducklings

JUDY CASELEY

These tiny egrets won't turn into swans. But, they'll grow up to be magnificent birds nonetheless. A species of the heron, the egret generally sports white plumage when fully developed.

2

A Frightened Foursome

JUDY CASELEY

Sensing danger, these white tail deer stand still and listen carefully at the Big Cypress Swamp. The swamp is near the Big Cypress Seminole Indian Reservation. At the reservation, Indians share their folk-lore and legends with visitors from around the world.

3

Baby Bird

FELIX KROCK
NIKON N 90
TAMERON, 70-300

Though he's young, this yellow crowned night heron can count on his instincts to tell him what to do when danger approaches. Aware that someone is watching him, he freezes and doesn't make a peep until he feels safe again.

1
Holding Pattern

CATHERINE LATIMER

A butterfly appears ready for take-off, after getting a power boost from the nectar of this blooming plant. His wings are spread, showing off beautiful bands and dots of color.

2
Turtle Love

JUDY CASELEY

Loggerhead turtles are caught mating in the Gulf of Mexico near Chokoloskee Island. The photographer stumbled upon these magnificent creatures while on a fishing trip offshore.

3
One With Nature

FRED WICKE
NIKON N 70
SEATTLECHROME 100
F 3.8 – 11, WITH BRACKETING

You don't have to plant your own garden to appreciate nature in Naples. Here, a butterfly flutters its wings on a thistle off U.S. 41, a major thoroughfare that connects Naples to the East Coast.

2

3

1

Snack Time

CAROLINE BROWN
NIKON F 100
300 MM LENS

After staking out his prey, a blue heron reels in a tasty morsel. The crawfish helplessly dangled from the bird's mouth, until he was gobbled up.

2

Bird of Paradise

HENRY NELL
OLYMPUS OMPC
KODAK GOLD AND EKTACHROME

These dazzling flowers appear to be in flight, and that's how they derive their name. The plant is native to Africa, but can be found in other spots with tropical climates, such as Naples.

3

Rocky Road

MARYLE BARBÉ
CANON EOS
KODAK 200

Perched on a rock early in the morning, a snowy egret ogles his surroundings. The bird, which has a wing span of about 38 inches, can be found lurking near mudflats, marshes and other shallow waters.

2

3

Pretty in Pink

ARLENE TALIADOROS

A Hibiscus tree, growing along a driveway in Pelican Marsh, blooms frequently, producing pink-colored beauties. Hibiscus trees and shrubs can be found in many backyards in Naples.

Bug Eyed Butterfly

CAROLINE BROWN
NIKON F-100 60 MM LENS

A butterfly stands at attention after detecting a human in this otherwise peaceful garden. Though small, this courtyard garden has all sorts of plants and flowers, from orchards and ferns to petunias and pink sage.

1

2

1	2	3
Nature's Way	**Afternoon Delight**	**Flower Power**
ARLENE TALIADOROS NIKON N-90 FUJI 400	ARLENE TALIADOROS NIKON N-90-S FUJI COLOR	CAROLINE BROWN NIKON F 100 80-200 LENS
Resting on rocks, this cactus catches the eye of those lucky enough to visit this private garden in Kings Lake.	A double hibiscus flower begins to unfold. With a little help from Mother Nature, its petals will soon stretch out fully, an awesome sight.	A beautiful brugmansia, also known as an angel trumpet, blooms in a back-yard garden in Pelican Bay. The green thumb is Caroline's mother Christine, who says the garden is "stuffed with plants" and is always changing.

3

1

2

1

Snake Eyes

HERMAN MOLL
EOS A 2
VELVIA

Water moccasins, also known as cottonmouths, can be found lurking in the swamps in Southwest Florida. The slow-moving snake has a vicious bite, but it's rarely fatal.

2

Ready to Take the Plunge

WANDA SOLON
KODAK 35 MM 200 SPEED

One. Two. Three. A grasshopper appears ready to take a jump at the Corkscrew Swamp Sanctuary, a world-renowned national preserve.

1

2

1

Open Up, and Say Ah

JUDY CASELEY

An alligator fiercely defends his territory. It's creatures like this that made the Disney-owned Caravan/Hollywood Pictures crew nervous during the filming of *Gone Fishin'*. The film was made on the western edge of the Everglades, just off U.S. 41.

2

Tricks for Treats

JUDY CASELEY

Using the sun as his spotlight, a raccoon shows off in hopes of getting a snack. During a swamp buggy ride, you'll see raccoons close up. For a few marshmallows, they'll do all sorts of tricks.

1

2

3

1

Gotcha!

FELIX KROCK
NIKON N 70
TAMERON 70 – 300 LENS AT 300 MM
STUDIO 35, KODAK ROYAL GOLD 200

A hungry bird catches his prey on a lettuce lake at Marsh Trail, a 6,825-acre preserve open seven days a week. A five-mile hiking path takes visitors through pine flatwoods, sawgrass marsh and oak and cabbage palm hammocks.

2

Fresh and Fruity

ARLENE TALIADOROS
NIKON N 90
FUJI 400

Thousands of acres of citrus groves enwrap the rural neighborhoods of the county. Canker, a highly contagious disease, has threatened to wipe out the citrus industry, not just locally but statewide. Here, the fruit appears nice and healthy.

3

Close to Extinction

JUDY CASELEY

A Florida panther scopes out his territory, looking for his next meal. He's one of only about 40 that live in the wild today.

1

1

Three's Company

MARYLE BARBÉ
CANON EOS
KODAK 200

Wood storks keep each other company as golfers make their way to the third hole. In Naples, golf is a favorite pastime. The area ranks second in the nation for the number of golf holes per resident.

2

Basking in the Sun

SUSAN MILLER
MINOLTA MAXXUM 400 SI
TAMERON AF100-300 MM
KODAK GOLD 200/FULL AUTO MODE

A gator warms himself in the sun along Jane's Scenic Drive in the Fakahatchee State Preserve, which stretches 72,000 acres. The alligator is not to be mistaken for a crocodile, which has a more pointed snout and an overbite.

3

Fly Away

MARYLE BARBÉ
CANON EOS
KODAK 200

A tiny green heron, dwarfed by his surroundings, squatted in these reeds for just a few minutes. Then he was gone again, flying off in search of a more interesting terrain.

2

3

1

2

1	2	3
What Did you Say?	**A Leg Up**	**Strike a Pose**
FRED WICKE NIKON N 70 SEATTLECHROME 100	FELIX KROCK NIKON N-90 TAMERON 70-300 LENS	RICHARD MADURA CANON SURESHOT KODACOLOR 200 AUTO FOCUS
An egret appears to have missed part of a conversation, as he was wading in shallow waters looking for fish. Either that or he had an itch. This bird, a great egret, is about 40 inches long.	A white ibis lifts his leg, preparing to take a step closer to its prey.	A pelican models for a cameraman, standing tall on a seawall in Marco Island, a quaint island south of Naples.

1
2

1

Under Construction

CARL STOYE

An Osprey flies in building materials, as his mate stands guard at the front door. Ospreys love to feed on fish, and their presence indicates that there are healthy waterways nearby. When they go fishing, they can make quite a splash as they dive into shallow waters to catch their prey.

2

Eagle-eyed

JUDY CASELEY

Eagles are found high above the treetops. Local environmentalists fight to protect the powerful bird from encroaching development in Southwest Florida.

List of Contributors

Angela Antilia
429 3rd Ave. North
Naples, FL 34102
page 19

Babs Armour
411 West End Ave.
New York, NY 10024
page 76

Maryle Barbé
26119 Fawnwood Ct.
Bonita Springs, FL 34134
pages 9, 113, 122, 123

Deborah Borowski
301 Country Club Dr.
Naples, FL 34110
page 33

Bob Bradford
703 Henley Drive
Naples FL 34104
page 29

Caroline Brown
1009 Greystone Cir.
Morgantowm WV 26508
*pages 25, 26–27, 32, 35, 44,
51,. 85, 91, 112, 115, 117*

Judy Caseley
PO Box 114
Chokoloskee, FL 34138
*pages 11, 98, 99, 103, 104,
108(2), 111, 119(2), 121*

Catherine Christian
4103 Old Mill Rd.
Springfield OH 45506
pages 40–41

John Cicilline
705-4 August Nlvd.
Naples, FL34113
pages 18–19, 49, 100

Gene Clayton
4130 Bayhead Dr. #306
Bonita Springs, FL
pages 78–79

Cynthia Cronig
47 Lakeside Dr. East
Centerville, MA 02632
page 62

Roger Devore
Tryan Circle
LeBann, IL 62254-1948
pages 12–13

Ed Donaldson
555 Heron Point, St. Nicole
Naples, FL 34108
page 88

Ginny Folk
115 St. Stphen St. #42
Boston, MA 02115
pages 24, 76

Jackie Frank
Collier County Historical
pages 42–43

Eugene Gibbons
15161 Cedarwood Lane #
Napels, FL 34110
page 8

Marion Hammond
556 13th
Wood River, IL 62095
pages 31, 38

Nancy Hannigan
1089 Broad Ave. North
Naples, FL 34102
pages 58(2), 59, 61(2)

Marilyn Harris
3400 Gulf Shore Blvd.N. L-7
Naples FL 34103
page 75

Carolyn Hawkins
2065 W. Crown Pointe Blvd.
Naples, FL 34112
page 101

Samuel Hunkin II
PO Box 413005 PMB 32
Naples, FL 34101-3005
*pages 1, 3, 22, 84, 86–87, 88,
92, 93*

Dehlia Hurst
4420 Beechwood Lake Dr.
Naples, FL 34112
page 72

Christa Jaegers
7718 Jewel Lane #203
Naples, FL 34109
pages 68, 71, 72

Carolyn Johnstone
755 1st Ave. North
Naples, FL 34102
pages 55

Felix Krock
12221 Kobart Rd.
Micnocqua, WI 54548
pages 108–109, 120, 124

Catherine Latimer
1103 Michigan Ave.
Naples, FL 34103
page 110

Jody Lesko
82201 Old Highway #418
Islamoranda, FL 33036
page 63

Richard Madura
130 June Ct.
Marco Island, FL 34145
page 125

Suzy Maynard
The Hill School
Pottstown, PA 19464
page 62

Susan Miller
190 14th St NE
Naples, FL 34120
page 123

Herman Moll
6166 Sea Grass Lane
Naples, FL 33999
page 118

William Moseley
760 Waterford Dr. #301
Naples, FL 34113
page 39

Harry & Diana Nell
1260 Rordon Ave.
Naples, FL 34103
pages 68, 70, 113

Peggy Paradise
640 Rudder Rd.
Naples, FL 34102
page 10

Kay Patton
4320 Beechwood Lake Dr.
Naples, FL 34112
page 47

Lynne Redmond
4401 Gulfshore Blvd. N. PH 3
Naples, FL 34103
pages 67, 80

Paul Reinhardt
15 Chateau Way
Naples, FL 34112
page 105

Lenora Rickner
9195 The Lane
Naples, FL 34109
page 90

Lynn Royal
5616 Wisperwood Blvd. #1103
Naples, FL 34110
page 67

Jerry Shelton
1120 Litleneck Ct. 46E
Naples, FL 34102
pages 21, 32, 81

Gary Shultz
4860 Napoli Dr.
Naples, FL 34103
pages 28, 89

Dorothy Skoluda
3255 E. Locust Dr.
Palmyra, IN 47154
pages 102–103

Ann Skoluda Hoagland
6360 Pelican Bay Blvd. #303C
Naples, FL 34108
page 81

Wanda Solon
440 Henley Dr.
Naples, FL 34104
*pages 21, 24, 52–53, 53(2),
54(2), 56(2), 57, 73, 75, 96,
97, 103, 118, 128*

Nelsine Spooner
20534 green Tree Court
Estero, FL 33928-2024
page 50

Helen Stallard
2121 Gulf Shore Blvd N. Apt.
Naples, FL 34102
pages 4, 66–67

Paul Stevens
4420 Gail Blvd.
Naples, FL 34104
pages 22, 106, 107

Carl Stoye
1080 Old Marco Lane
Marco island, FL 34145
pages 74, 93, 126

Gerry Sugarman
816 Bentwood Dr.
Naples, FL 34108-8203
page 80

Ryvanne Susser
3319 Lowry Rd.
L.A. CA 90027
pages 36–37, 38, 71

Arlene Taliadoros
35 John Wise Ave.
Essex, MA
*pages 17, 29, 85, 114,
116(2), 120*

Carl Thome
937 4th Ave. South
Naples, FL 34102
page 60

Nancy Thurston
2150 Gulf Shore Blvd. North
Naples, FL 34102-1624
page 40

Lawrence Tomsic
7186 Mill Run Cir.
Naples FL 34109
pages 48, 77

August Uttich
5725 Gage Ln. Apt.305A
Naples, FL 34113-3578
pages 6–7, cover

Edie Vassamillet
113 Calais Ct.
Naples, FL 34112
page 46

Peter Wagner
240 Palm Dr. #4
Naples, FL 34112
pages 105

Lee Warner
6375 Old Mahogany Ct.
Naples, FL 34109
page 23

Barbara Wenderski
2421 Millcreek Ln #204
Naples, FL 34119
page 69

Fred Wicke
535 Broad Ave. South
Naples, FL 34102
pages 20–21, 30, 31, 111, 124

Tim Zello
7784 Emerald Cir. #201
Naples, FL 34109
page 45